To everything
there is a season

Jean Medcalf

By the same author

An emptiness beside me
A small circle of time

Cover illustration by John Minton, reproduced from 'A Country Heart' © Royal College of Art, used with permission

First published in 2012
By Lulu.com

A CIP record for this book is available from the British Library

ISBN 978-1-4716-5380-3

DEDICATION

To my parents, Bess and Bill Croft,
who brought me up and educated me.
To my husband Gordon and our children, Sally,
Lucy and Roger, who make all things possible.
And to my dear friend Iris Berry,
who always understood.

CONTENTS

Spring

Summer

Autumn

Winter

Spring

NEW YEAR

Midnight tolls
A flock of bells peals out
Swinging on a clapper
We fly
Backwards and forwards
Higher and higher
Soaring and swooping
Till
Balanced like birds on the upstroke of twelve
We poise
And dive
With courage into a virgin year.

February : lipchap nipnose dripnose
Frostbite chilblains and boys' mauve knees;
February: steam breath ice crack hoarfrost
Fern windows leaf rime and falling silent snow.

February: crunchgrass snowcreak stiffmud
Stonesong on iceponds; sheets rigid on the line;
February: hot toast warm slippers muffins
Coalfires scorched legs and pictures in the flames.

February: hotmitts earmuffs greatcoats
Balaclava helmets and warm woolly vests;
February: snowdrops primrose crocus
Blacktwigged almond blossom, pink before the leaf.

February: Candlemas purify expiate
Barebranch stripbare nothing to hide;
Daffodils greenspear upthrust through the earth
Trees deciduous decide to bud again.

FLOURISH

While clearing out my shed some weeks ago
I found some bulbs
Stunted, forgotten, past their "plant by "date
Every gardener knows what I mean.
I held them in my hands, weighing, cogitating
Were they worth the trouble of planting?
Would knife straight stems grow
from curvy shoots?
I considered.

Give us a chance, the crocuses seemed to plead
So I did, planted them into pots,
And let the sun do its work.
Some weeks later
Sunlight and earth makes plants grow straight,
I found

Give everything another chance to see the light
Yourself included

PRIMAVERA

Glancing greenly from black branches
Slim tight buds begin to show
Royal purple crocus blazon
Honey tongued with dusky glow
Lavender crocus, blue threaded
Shout from chalky pencilled leaves
Furry fingered palm leaves beckon;
Primroses and violets weave
Patterns in the brightening hedgerows
Aquilegia furled unfurl
Leaves that have been curled uncurl
Headlong movement all around us
Tells us what we shall receive
Movement all around us headlong
Spring runs fast, we must believe

FIVE FLOWERS FROM THE CZAR

When we first moved here, thirty years ago,
We thought that you were dead,
Massacred by your previous owner.

But we waited, and in time
Over the years you put out green shoots,
Grew flowers and showered us with fruit.

I picked plums from your branches, made jam,
My children climbed your trunk -
You were a home to nesting blue tits.

Last year, without warning, you dropped a bough
When you were heavy with plums,
To indicate that you were very old.

Surgery became necessary;
Men came with chain saws, and I thought - again-
They'd killed you and grew sad.

We found holes in your heart-wood
Your trunk was split
But luckily your roots took strength from clay.

****

Today in yellow March,
Springing from your amputation,
I saw - with joy - five white flowers tremulous.

Now in your sixtieth year
You can still surprise us -
Show us how to survive and be renewed
even though
You once nearly lost heart.

CITY SPRING

Who can work while the Spring
Colours the blossoming air with its scent
Unrest uprising fills the atmosphere
Only bricks and mortar stand static

Sap running, rising up in triumph
Rushing to fill our tired bodies with new life
We yawn, stretch and wake
Draw breath again and crawl from hibernation.

Grey winter trees grow green
Forgotten sun dazzles our dull eyes
From the earth spring flowers –
From the dusty bulbs crocus and snowdrops flash

Earth yields anew – hard pavements only grow
Torn paper and burnt matchsticks
Grey bricks stay grey
The typist wears a bunch of yellow primroses

No sprouting buds for townsmen
Iron girders and chimney posts stretch
Cold and angry fingers to the sky
Neon signs our flowers – traffic our nightingales

DAFFODILS

I love the name of daffodil
It is like the flower itself
Crisp and precise
Yet with a hint of coquetry
And frilliness

I should like to be a daffodil
Like a demure sentinel of the Spring
Martial yet wanton
Unbending in its stem, but
Tossing its fresh starched trumpet
Into the cool caressing breeze

MOVEABLE FEAST – EASTER, ST JOHN'S

Sorry, God
I've not been to see You
For so long – until Today
Forgive me

I'd forgotten the beauty of Communion
Forgotten the peace of God
which passeth all understanding
Forgotten the Paschal Candle
The Paten and the Chalice, the wafer and the wine,
The height of the church where I was confirmed
It was like coming home

Take, eat, this is my Body which is given for you
This is my Blood of the New Testament
Do this in remembrance of me

I'd not presumed to come to thy Holy Table.
Like Martha,
I'd been cumbered about with much serving
I'd been careful and troubled about many things
Family, friends, house, dog, garden.
I'd forgotten that good part, the needful thing

But now I've remembered, presumed and returned
Now I'm back
I won't leave it
So long
Next time.

MAY

Like a girl in a party dress
Pink as a blush
The apple tree now rains petals
As confetti falls at a wedding.

Later, the bees all gone,
The tree stands quietly waiting.

In autumn, pregnant with apples,
It stands heavy laden
Like a girl, finished blushing,
Great with child.

Summer

LUXEMBOURG

Barefoot through dewy grass
We walked to bathe
Deep in the river; the cool dawn air
Moved slowly as if loath to stir the leaves
Which gently clothe the branches of the trees.
Far church bells swang in muffled beauty from
A distant abbey; birds began to sing.
A sudden swallow swooped; a flash of blue
Blended into the sky and disappeared.
Tranquil, the water crystalled at my feet
Reflecting silently all I hold dear -
A clarity of sky, a sense of peace -
I listened; the earth paused and held its breath.

Returned now - in homecoming lies pity -
I cannot hear the silence in the city.

WEST MERSEA

Illuminated by the lucent moon
The satin mudbanks shine on either side
The river, as with creaking oars we row
Coolly upstream at night. The gentle breeze
Ruffles our hair and slaps the tiny waves
Gently against our boat. The mirrored moon,
Splintered by oar-strokes, runs to coalesce
Like mercury spilt. Tall withies bend quiet heads
In slender benediction, as we pass
Double-reflected ships with star-ringed masts.
A plaintive bird sings a lament, a sweet
And solitary air; we rest our oars.

Blackwater - silvered - flows on without pause.
Over our tired heads the darkness falls.

QUESTION AND ANSWER

Anxious
I asked my friendly oak
About the child
My son had given
To a girl I hardly knew

It listened solidly
My acorns often grow
Far from me
Carried by squirrels and the wind
I do not see their youth

I only know
What is in me will be in them
Have faith
Have patience
What is in you will be in her

TAKE AND GIVE

Last Sunday afternoon we took a walk
My family and I
Plus, for the first time, Victoria.

We fed the ducks, then walked into the woods.
I found a chestnut tree - as is my wont
I put my arms around it for loving help.
It took from me my fears and uncertainties
And gave to me tranquillity and love

I said goodbye and turned to walk away
And as I did I saw my actions copied.
Like a small bright butterfly clinging to the trunk,
Face pressed to the bark, a small girl
Laughed in imitation of her grandmother.

She took nothing from the tree
But gave to it her sparkling love of life
Her joy and champagne laughter.

She was so small as to be near the roots.
Her brightness will be stored
In readiness for future visitors
Seeking hope, and calm, and love.

DEBDEN HOUSE

The morning of the year awakens me
The forest beckons me with silent voice
My dog and I, all senses open wide
Both toil up hill into an unknown land

Knowing no landmarks, shall I leave behind,
Like babes in wood, a trail of crumbled bread
Tot make my path against my safe return
Or trust to memory alone to serve?

A beech invites; I settle in its roots
Textured like elephant hide, rough to my hand.
Its branches umbrella me from rain
I hold the beechmast tightly like a charm.

Around, the beeches vault a blue roofed church
A leafy wall shields brightness from the sun
Windshaken branches sprinkle holy drops
In font-like benison on those below.

A squirrel undulates across the earth
A sinuous grey caterpillar he,
Abrupt, transfixed by thoughts of food unfound
Buried years deep in leaf mould underground

My stick digs years deep in leafy mould
The squirrels eat nuts for all time
And the wind in the leaves like the sound of the sea
As I turn and return to the house that welcomes me

LAVENDER PATCH

When the bees leave
That's my sign

Snip snip with the shears
Snip snip cutting the sun
Stored in the heavy grain

When the bush was newly planted
It stood in the furthest part of the bed
Each summer as I snipped
I saw that it had moved
Reaching to the sun, the sun

Touching each visitor
Welcome or not
Brushing their legs with its heads
Scented, scented

Moving and touching is what it does -
now it finally covers the path, the path,
Deterring the unwelcome
Scenting the beloved

And each summer I wait for the bees
To finish their work.
Then I start mine.
Snip, snip – into the lavender bags
Storing the sun.

Autumn

HEARTWOOD

Upwards soars my head to Heaven,
Deep my roots dug firm in clay;
Squirrels eat my acorns dropping,
In my branches build their dreys.
Lovers carve true-love upon me -
Hearts and tokens in my bark.
Sun and Moon pour brightness on me;
I am the same by day or dark.

I saw crowned Queen Boadicea
Saw the Romans come and go;
Humans change, but I am constant;
Tree above, and they below.
Springtime sees my youth upon me,
Dropping autumn leaves me bare.
Winter lends me hoary fingers -
I change only with the year.

Humans: know my powers to comfort;
Know that I can bring you peace.
Tranquil rest your soul within me;
From all cares I give release.

If you put your arms around me,
Hug me round my crusty bark,
Troubled head to dusty roughness,
Touchwood close to unquiet heart –

Then my Heartwood self will bless you,
From your heavy fears absolve,
Draw them deep into my own roots,
Strengthen you with oak resolve.

Know then: we are one forever.
You shall be ours when you are clay.
Abiding, loving, green in spirit,
Remaining Dryads all our days.

SUNSET

The sunset came –
And like flicked spume
That runs along the edges of the waves
The orange yellow cloud
Combed out into the eyeblue sky
All was bathed in light –
Warm pinkish glow,
Gracious and mother of pearl
Ever changing and altering its tints
Deeper and redder as the dusk came down

The widening light spread sheer across the sky
In varying formations
Duller as it faded.
Like angels' wings, fanned wide
Athwart the heavens
Flaming proudly, tenderly down

BLAZE

God poured a paintbox through this tree
Spilt gilt, rinsed rust, tipped russet,
Flowed gold, splashed yellow, dripped carmine,
Flushed crimson, burnt orange, and with his brush
Stippled the fallen leaves with fire.

His spectrum red, His hues tawny,
Bright ruddy tints incarnadine the leaves
Shine coral, rosywarm, bronzeburn,
Glowing with stained glass clarity
His palette runs the gamut of autumn.

Incarnate colour stands this tree
Garlanded gold, magenta blushed, flame flooded,
Poppystain, honey-blazon, goldbright,
Beech burnished, hot glazed, foxy sheen -
An illuminated letter in a copper rubric of prayer.

LATE BEAUTY

From my bedroom window
I can see into the heart of my tall old pear tree.
My father-in-law called it Doyenne du Comice
and said it must wed a Beurre Hardy.
Now in October
the Virginia creeper twines carmine
Blood red among the green pendant pears.
The creeper comes into its crimson beauty
in autumn.
At the height of its powers its leaves will drop
Suddenly to burnish the brown earth beneath

It is at the height of its beauty just before death

I wonder – is this how it will be with grandparents
Best just before death?

EVERGREEN

Beyond fertility
Beyond maturity
I consider my end
Will I burn in a fire?
Will I rot in the earth?
When I'm gone will they notice the gap?
Support and shelter I can still provide.
But for how much longer I do not know.
Support I need for myself now
Lest I fall prematurely to earth.

I have done my best to be a good tree
Grown tall
Done no-one any harm
Never violated my earth space

But trees do not live forever.
Not even a eucalyptus

AUTUMN

Slowly the old man bends to the steamy soil
Forks up to the smoky sun the fertile loam

From the beginning he has known
his allotment of earth
But will not know til the end
his allotment of time.

Winter

DEATH OF THE CZAR

I told them I was ill
Warned them about the ivy strangling me
Told them I'd lost heart
Was rotten to the core
But no-one heeded me
They preferred the bullace, the starry stranger.
I'd done my best for seventy years
Carefully watched over the man, the woman,
The children, the many dogs and visitors
Gave them many pounds of juicy plums

But now – I'd had enough.
I hate the snow, the ice got in my trunk,
needling my bark
The rain bent me and took my strength away

But the last straw
Was that bloody grey squirrel
Always jumping on my sore branch tip
I'll show him, I thought.
I'll bide my time
I won't hurt the woman or the dog
Or the fence, they cost

But the grey won't bother me again
Bloody immigrant!

Crunch! Crash! Tear! Rip!
Over at last!   All gone dead!
Chainsaw time.

WINTERSONG

I heard somebody playing my tune today
A boy standing by my pond was singing my song

Unheard by me for fifty years.

He was playing my
"Stonesong on icepond" song
Skimming stones skilfully across the ice
Singing as they resounded
Echoing from the water under the ice
Singing, skimming, sliding, shirring –
A sound unheard in any place
Or any other time

"It only works on ice" he muttered
"Thanks for talking to me."

A lanky inarticulate adolescent
Bored with throwing stones
But finally finding his inner voice
Unknown until frozen.

SEEN FROM A TRAIN

A white blizzard
Needling the skin
Horizontally

In the corner of the white cemetery
By the angel of death
Six black figures
Curving
Six black umbrellas
Shielding
Their faces from hail and grief
Surrounding
The black hole

Patterning
The white earth
Six red wreaths
Like blood
Spilling

SNOW

The earth has drawn her ermine fur about
Her shoulders: from her leafy hair the dropping
Icicles glisten, backgrounded by black branches
Frosty diamonds dazzle in her dress.

White days, white nights, white loves
No colour in the whiteness of her gown
None but the moon to bear her company
Whose touch silvers her skirts

Star-dusted dreamers wander hand in hand
Through the white night; caught in a web
Of frosted mesh of magic softly they go.
Bells in the breeze weave melodies over their head.

Gently the earth lets drop the ermine wrap,
Puts off her jewels, warms to the touch of the sun.
The moon fades in the sky and dreamers wake.
Winter retreats – green spring is coming near

SONNET

Mistletoe hangs in milky clusters now -
  Each house aglow with colour; deep and dark
    Reds predominate. In the holly bough
      Ruby shine berries, paint bright in the bark
        Yule logs flame in the hearth, vermilion
          edged.

Curtains fold crimson, close against the night,
High stars flare in the Christmas tree, and hedged
Round with bright tinsel, brilliant globes of light
In gold and silver sparkle. In the lanes
  Softly in velvet whiteness falls the snow.
    The frost appears fernwhite on windowpanes
      Music rings out as carol-singers go
        Along by moonlight; children, their
          stockings near,
            Sleep in their drowsy beds. Christmas is
              here.

INDEX OF FIRST LINES

About the Author

Jean Medcalf was born in East London in 1931. She has been writing poetry since the age of 14.

She was a prizewinner in the annual Forward Press Top 100 Poets competition 2003, coming second from over 50,000 entries. Her poems have been published in several anthologies.

She recently co-wrote with her daughter Sally a verse play, 'Mother's Runaway Daughter' about her mother's life in East London during two World Wars.

Her poetry is emotive and frequently inspired by her love of nature and trees. Many of them relate to the theme of the unending cycle of life; birth and death, childhood, marriage, motherhood, and growing old.

Her influences include Rupert Brooke, Walter de la Mare, Edward Thomas, and Stephen Spender.